RUCHI CHANDAN

First Published in November 2021

ISBN: 978-93-5472-174-8

BLUEROSE PUBLISHERS

www.bluerosepublishers.com

info@bluerosepublishers.com

+91 8882 898 898

Cover Design:

Swati Singh

Typographic Design:

Jyoti

Distributed by: Blue Rose, Amazon, Flipkart

In honor of

Akhand Dhuna

Dera Baba Rudranand Ashram

Vill-Nari, District- Una (HP)

Shri Shri1008 Dera Baba Rudranand Ji
Maharaj Una (HP)

(Ved-veta, Tapomurti, Bhramnisht,
Vedantacharya Param-pujya)

Shri Shri 1008 Sugrivanand Ji Maharaj
Una (HP)

Dedication

This book is dedicated in the sweet remembrance of my father Advocate Bimal Chandan "Bitta" (1964-2014),
Lt col Anita Mehta my inspiring mother & my beloved brother Nishchal Chandan a passionate footballer

Contents

1
The Queen of Wands

"You are power"

No one calls you honey,
when you are sitting on the throne
you are the fire which can burn down the floors
when you are the power,
it's not yours to give away the crown.
when you are not made for any,
but the crown is meant for you all
why behave like wolves when you ascend from the lions!
your lineage is different, so behave like them
because the one who owns the fire can never be frozen
then standing alone in the pack of wolves, will not matter
so you stand your grounds with the crown
then no one can sweep you off your feet,
even if they want
because I am fire & the lion and I am the Queen of Wands.

QUEEN of WANDS.

2
Absolutely not

"Donating is a noble deed, but to donate your power is not a noble job, be it for love, fear or healing"

Be conscious,
don't drain yourself in emotions
learn to claim your power in every situation,
it doesn't mean to fight anyone
it means to claim your power within
so no one can overrun you
or take you for granted
so learn, not to give away your power to anyone
build yourself from scratch
to keep your head high
learn to rise from the ashes
then you can burn an endless number of times
don't let anyone press their fears, strength or opinions over you
specially in love,
don't over involve yourself in another
my life is yours & yours is mine, is the basic crap
so stop shitting your own life
because one will always overpower the other,
as soon as you over involve,
then the real problems begin

to be happy throughout the journey, set your boundaries straight
so no one takes the other for granted
because true love, liberates & if you are stuck
it's time to contemplate
it is easier to blame the other,
but it's not their fault, really
it's you who overstepped, who forgot the boundaries
love is unconditional but not at the condition of your soul
know your value first
have the integrity to say absolutely not,
so you don't drown yourself later
because water is life, till there is a dam
if the dam breaks, you know what will happen next
so don't put yourself in the same situations
life is teaching you not to be in every day
it's just a matter of realization,
you can find all your answers, if you look within.

3
Before you rise

"Choose the energies you want to be around, eliminate all kinds of draining situations from your life and energetically make shifts"

They undervalue you
they take you for granted
and step all over you
but now, that you are okay
when they see you standing on your feet
and see that you've made it
that your sorrow & painful experiences didn't let you crawl on the floor
now they are going to want to come back to you
now what to do?
obviously you can't disrespect them
or let your pride come in the way and make the decision for you
there is no need to accept them as well
so how to decide what's next?
you can use your power of discernment well
make sure these people really value you, now
make sure that the exchange of energy,
of what you give & receive is equal for you
that will help you decide
it's not that you have to let them go

but you need to express your emotions firmly & constructively too

don't let anyone take your energy away from you

so you can only have appreciative people around you

so now you decide

what energy you want to step into

the one which aligns with your higher self or the one that is draining you

know whom to be with & whom to let go.

4
Ascend

"Begin your ascension process, there is more than what meets the eye, let your intuition guide you to your higher call"

Surrender your ego
for accessing higher knowledge & understanding
be governed by the light, not by your shadows
ascend
from where you started, it counts
though you have elevated from those past energies
but they were a part of you once
so hold compassion for them who are still in those energies
you are not better,
you have just leveled up first
so pass no judgments
focus on your soul's evolution,
that you are now here in the physical
distinguish between the physical & the inner comfort
can you sit with yourself?
in stillness, are you content within or is there still something that you want
is there something still distracting you!
& if you get it, will you be done?
if not, ask yourself for what is it that you're here for

to gather physical & material wealth that's all?
is that the only worth of your time & soul!
to earn get busy & die!
stop running for a second
sit quietly & go within
stop confusing being busy with emptiness inside
if you take time and go slowly,
new perceptions will emerge, that you can't see if you move too fast
move away from rapidly moving in everyday life
& step into the zone of stillness
there is more to life,
than you have seen & created in your mind
only if you go within, will you be able to look beyond
so begin your ascension process now
by thinking & understanding things on a much deeper level then you are used to
push yourself out of your comfort zone
and don't let your mind run away from you.

5
Ask yourself

"Stop scratching the surface, lets understand the depth and come to the meaning behind sentences"

Why aren't we enough?
why can't we survive on our own and learn to fight and overcome our own battles first
what is it that makes us need another?
why can't we wait till we know and build ourselves first?
Is it because of our fears or we need support
or due to domestic traumas,
childhood traumas,
emotional wounds,
insecurities,
money,
intimacy,
ego
what is that you are so afraid off
that as soon as you step out in the world
you have the need to run towards another
to camouflage your emptiness with the presence of another
why do you feel depressed?
what is eating you?
where is that energy coming from?

what is the root cause?
how can you transmute your problems into strength?
Is it anyone's job to take your depression away
why don't you learn, how to come out of it & make
yourself such, that you never feel like that again
stop depending on others
and ask yourself the right questions
only if you recognize the reason will you be able to
find the solution,
to overcome your problems and win your battles
so someone as strong as you can come in,
and you both can be powerful together
instead of reversing the power in bringing the other
one up
and exhausting the energies, in reviving the
dependent
then there is no energy left to be powerful together
and then the one, rules the other
so stop exhausting the energy of another, in order to
bring yourself up
learn to live on your own
learn to survive,
learn to fight your battles, to stand your grounds
to feel content within
to be at bliss
to have something of your own
don't look out for things that are missing in you,
build those things in yourself first
otherwise problems will soon knock your doors
it's all about realization

but if you are happy, feeding the energy of another
then there is really not much anyone can say
no judgments from this side
but I don't see a point in living like a parasite
but it is a choice that only you can make
if you want to stand on your own or just feed off like a parasite.

6
Bring it on

"Master the art of discernment"

Bring it on
let them hate you
let them be jealous
& send all their negative & self -absorbed energies towards you
never give too much energy to these people,
who don't have your best intentions at heart
master the art of discernment
let the whole god-damn world be against you
let them fall as down as they want to
you need not care
it's their job to step on another
learn to defend & protect yourself
learn how to cleanse
ground your energies and channel them well
learn to transmute every bad energy that is sent your way
stand your grounds
let no one shake them
learn defense, it is essential
not only physical but energetic defense as well
as soon as you can
take the responsibility of your mind, body & soul

so nothing can harm you &
nothing can come your way
build physical & energetic boundaries around you
entangle from everything that doesn't evolve you
let them come,
but before that learn to transmute all negative energies into positive for you
don't let those self- absorbed energies make you feel small
kick them out, as soon as they enter your zone
the ones who put out bad energies for others will get them back as well
it takes a whole amount off toll on their energies too
so don't you worry
let their karma take care of them
you focus on protecting & dissolving yours
there are many tools out there in the world
that can help
but beware to not discard or involve just in anything as you like
follow proper guidance & take instructions first,
so you don't harm yourself more.

7
Choice

"Ego or wisdom"

Which energy will you choose to guide you?
embrace your tiger energy
you are fierce & courageous too
even though you have the power to attack
but before you do,
take a moment
to be still & quiet for a while
observe the environment around you
it is great if you are powerful
but don't let it come from the loud noise of ego inside of you
don't let it overpower the soft voice of wisdom in you
learn to center yourself before you attack, if it is really needed to
give a moment, to the wisdom in you
that's owning your power
by not letting your emotions rule you
but you ruling them
so when you attack,
make sure it is for the right reasons & do it without belittling the other
speak your truth of course
but with the fair leader inside you

don't let your integrity & grace fall away when you attack
it is graceful when you have power with integrity
otherwise pride will make you misuse it
which is not good for growth!
so walk your talk before you really address
surrender your ego to yourself
so you can live your life as you wish to
with your power in alignment with you
and don't be scared of the power you hold
just let your wisdom guide you that's all
only the strongest knows when & how to work their emotions
it doesn't mean you suppress them,
just listen to your wisdom above everything else.

8
Codependency

"Let others follow the same agreement you have made to yourself"

Physical, emotional or whatever
make yourself such
as if you are the ultimate person you are looking for
you need no one to be your rescuer
to be the hero or your leader,
as a divine connection in your life
go within first &
make yourself as the best partner you can get in the universe
let go off the feeling of wanting to be codependent
recognize & stand in your power
you have the potential within you
grow beyond gender
this limited perception of you
we all have both the feminine & the masculine energy within us
nurture your feminine energy using your masculine energy & vice versa
set the intention to know & grow first
and when you have done the work
only then you are truly ready to look for another soul,
whom you want to call your own

until then,
spend time with you, so you can sit & hear yourself
commit, love, respect & honor oneself
so anyone who comes in your life
follows the same agreement that you have made to yourself
there is no need to be codependent
be your individual self, first.

9
Cut the cords

"Stop breathing in the old & breathing out new"

Stop living in the past & thinking of the future
know who you are & how to handle your energies
cut the threshold & come into the new way of being
because it doesn't work that way
what you have, you have it right now
what you want, you have within
there is no perfect day to come
you may not be alive tomorrow
so what is it that you're going to take with you?
don't waste your life thinking of old or new
what is done is done
what is to come, you don't know
even if it will come, you have no clue
so don't live in your perceived mistakes
what happened was just a lesson, what is to come, you are yet to learn
this is just life,
it happens to all of us
you did what you thought was best at the time
you're no special than any other you can think off
you might be unaware of their problems but everyone is experiencing their part
nobody is born wise, you become wise

what you make of your experiences, that makes you wise,
enlightened people are not born enlightened,
they seek & work on themselves,
they work on that, which is not taught in school or college books, they do the work of life
put intentions out for the future but appreciate what you have now,
to start feeling good just as you are, is also an art
how much ever you accomplish, it will never be enough
so enjoy, how far you have come
you are an amazing soul, just as you are
there are many, who want the life you have right now
it is the opinion that limits you
so go on self -discovery mode now
so you can be content & smile even through your problems
& fulfil all your duties without getting attached or expecting anything from anyone
do what is to be done
life will happen to you with a much better scale than you can ever think off
every step of your journey counts, every step was a lesson you needed to learn
your journey to now & within will change everything around
so cut cords of was & will & come to now.

10
Dare to feel

"Dare to feel & not get carried or drowned away" it's a challenge.

Choose truce
accept the flaws & make everything work
choose to meet half way
and not go into extremes
don't get caught up in between right or wrong, black or white
just take the middle path
which will lead you to more balance & sense
put your energy into something constructive
it is not about choosing right or wrong
it's about embracing both, vice versa
light doesn't exist without dark
choose the middle path and let things flow
trust & let your emotional healing take place
not everything every time is sun & shinny
also learn how to embrace your dark & gloomy
let your heart heal
if it heals everything else will balance itself out
so become like a sponge
and clear your heart space from all blockages
go slow, take your time
every feeling you have is valid

so, allow yourself to feel your feelings
do not dismay them
every emotion is an energy which needs to be
expressed & experienced,
so it does not cause a blockage in you
we are the conduits of energy
so don't suppress your emotions,
otherwise
blocking your channels will cause problems & an
imbalance in you
so feel any feeling that you have, even if it pains
if it's hurting, it means, it is supposed to
endings are always painful & learning is supposed to
hurt
physically & in brain it happens
accommodation & strengthening is painful
& takes its own time too
so never give up
you need to push yourself through
so you don't get stuck in the process for long
give yourself positive affirmation as well
experience it,
let it course through you
then go within
so it can pass through
like a sponge, release all that is not meant to
feelings bring out your true self that is true
but not what it makes the others think
but what is it that you are experiencing & reacting
out off

because obviously you're hurting
that's where it's coming from,
balance out, so you can have a better quality of life
an emotional mind & heart needs peace
"embrace the in between" by not choosing
you need to flow by not forcing
so take time off but don't drown in your feelings.

11
Discern gracefully

"If you allow yourself to see, you really see"

Accept situations & people as they truly are
without denying the difficulties
only then when you really see,
make the best decision
by seeing how it makes you feel
discern it
there are only souls around you
only with different levels of consciousness, that's all
you are no better than the other, just ahead of
someone or maybe behind
who knows!
so focus on your path
which one is it that you want
leave whatever doesn't serve you
it's okay if you are not willing to stand it
there is no compulsion
but make sure to free yourself from the slavery of
your opinions too
be there or don't that's your personal choice
but do not pass judgements
what do you know about the experiences, the other
person has been through!
you are nobody to judge

look at everyone with compassion and love
and if you can't
the least you can do, is to leave it be
without lowering your soul's integrity
so if you don't like something
have the integrity to walk away gracefully
there is no need to create a mess where there is no need for it.

12
Dissolve

"The soul needs nourishment too, the only boundary which you need to dissolve is between you and the spirit"

Dissolve the boundaries between you & the universe
awaken the sense of oneness within you
start connecting to everything around you
tap into the sense of universal at-one-ness
if you truly connect, you will know
you've never been alone & you shall never be
speak freely to the plants & animals around
even they can hear the vibrations of your loving worlds
they too uplift when shown
gratitude & appreciation
for dissolution of self
take steps towards the universe
but first let nature help you & heal you on the cellular level
know the importance of your soul,
sit still & beyond ego
don't let the opinions of any define you
only you know your soul's call
to know the deepest part of your being,
you need to be willing to understand what has brought you to this point

& no one can do it for you
but before that, your soul needs nourishment too
so do right by you,
before you exhaust all the life energies within you
let your journey in the physical strengthen your relationship with the universe
so you can align with your higher purpose.

Dissolution of self leads to the infinite potential within you

13
Don't complicate

"Don't fight a battle that you are losing to yourself"

You don't have any control on life
all you have control over is yourself
life will happen to you, the way it wants to
you can only decide your response for what comes your way
when things happen to you, beyond your control
move away from what was & move to something new
shed the old skin & let the new come to you
just focus to master your particular vessel which has been given to you
because that's all you have control over
how you respond to life, how you manage
where your energies go & your boundaries
how can you overcome difficulties!
what are you here for
is there something that you are missing out on?
answers will come if you ask the right question
so ask yourself
what is it in you that needs change!
don't over complicate your life for all the reasons you have absolutely no control over
there is no point in arguing that
we are all here for our soul's evolution

and we will get all that we have signed up for
so no matter what happens, learn & strengthen yourself from within each day
win yourself over, be in control of your emotions
so you pass unaffected through whatever situation life brings over
the universe is not in your control
so don't worry about how life is going to happen for you
but how are you going to handle it, should be your goal.

14
Ego

"Take ego's wit away"

Ego is a tricky little monster
it will tell you whatever things that you are going to buy into
to keep you, small
so you do not claim yourself, your truth as a soul,
because the moment that you begin to really break away
from the thinking, thoughts and the ego's block
& step into the truth of who you are,
the ego's wit has to die
ego is like the dog that thinks he is the master
so get past that place
from limited to limitless
there is nothing that you cannot do as soon as you claim it in your heart & soul
break free from the illusions that are blocking you
create a new color or do whatever the hell you want to
let nothing come in your way
take your eyes off the future & pull your vision to play
figure out the first step & go after it
life is not a movie that you can watch just now
clarity will come each day

look at the little steps & not the whole picture at once
accomplish little by little
& confidence will come
it doesn't come immediately for everyone
it builds, in time
you are able, you are worthy
everything will happen within time
but do it from a place of passion
value the gift that you have
without letting your ego guide you either which way.

15
Energy

"Master your energy, from there comes power, with great power comes great responsibility"

Untangle your energies
from all that which consumes it
become aware of where you are channeling it
know it's worth
is it strengthening or depleting
are you using it for your growth or just throwing it away
become aware first
then untangle them
stay away from all dark energies
be it thoughts or your surroundings
protect it from all that, which takes it away
replenish it then,
even if you don't know anything
nature, solitude & stillness will serve the best way
gather your energies by surrounding yourself with higher vibrational beings
& then balance them out
put it to use with full consciousness
so everything else falls in place
energies need a good amount of inner work too
the tools are simple

but to trust the process in on you
because it is a slow process, but meaningful too
once you get into it,
it doesn't relapse every now and then
only with awareness can you do something about it
then slowly & firmly you can raise your vibrations
which will help you take the next step towards your soul's evolution here
for what you make space, you attract the same
so make sure your energy is on point always.

16
Faith

"The truest of devotion is usually unseen by many"

Overcome conflict with your resilience
resilience & obstacles are only preparations
for greater accomplishments
trust in self,
build strength
while learning through the contrast & chaos
have faith that you can be in a mix of chaos & still know that you can get it together
I believe it will get better, is strength
wisdom will come
to believe the impossible you got to be someone strong
because the people with the most powerful destinies, are tested hard
even till the last,
you cannot give up
your light should not be compromised in any situation, no matter what
only then the tables will turn in your favor
& right before your eyes,
the universe will turn even the negative in your favor
every set back into your success
all good that you put out, will come right back to you

even when it seems nothing is working for you
at that time see where your plans are seeded and what energy are you making decisions from
it's just delayed unfolding that's all
so never give up faith
in the highest of souls, the divine alone
no matter what form or shape you want to surrender to
but your faith & devotion should be ultimate
not by showing anyone will you have it
it's about your soul's intention & energy that counts
where it really matters, your every little deed does,
because the truest of devotion is usually unseen by many
but for that you need to put that amount of intensity & energy into something
only if you believe, it will happen for you.

17
Find love inside

"Strong journey back to self"

Love is all I thought I want
I couldn't love me
so I tried to find it around
the whole purpose of life was to find love of someone I thought
but now I realize, it was my love that I needed the most
what a mess I created,
till I found that out
everything happens for a reason, now I know
such a turbulent life
I walked slowly, but right
time took my tests time & again, so I can learn my lessons well
& set my boundaries straight
so I can reach where I am meant to be
even though the mice energy still comes around
but now, even the troubles look sweet
I'm still glad to reach here finally,
the answers I found were not easy to achieve
contemplation & healing are not at all easy
it takes an immense amount of energy
but I learned the hard way

by acceptance & surrendering
now I am where I wanted to be
no money or else's love has brought me here
but my strength to fight & overcome
my problems & pain
and still, I did not get bitter on the way
love, patience, compassion & wisdom are keys
no matter what tasks life brought
I found myself rising from misery,
resilience is my power my ultimate one
on the way, I found me & what is it that I want
though there is a lot more, yet to unfold
but I know I will get it together
no matter from what height I fall,
I will build myself again
I will always stand my ground with integrity and
power & faith in my spirit alone.

18
Flow

"Little change in doing little things everyday can change your energy completely"

It is not always a linear road
be ready for the twists & turns
a leap of faith is needed at times
maybe you are being tested or
you're being asked to believe at this time
so don't be closed off to your spirit
step into the sense of duality
make your decisions based on frequency
delays are not always bad
don't rush around
to fill your voids
you need not prove anything to anyone
all you need is your approval & that's all
you need to flow through this life
we need not be using or hurting one other, the way we are
that way we are just undermining our soul
there are better ways to do every day task
from talking to doing, every little thing
become such that whatever you see
becomes beautiful
whatever you touch turns to gold

use your wisdom to lay down your burdens
the way forward goes step by step
allow everything in your life to flow
it will so, if you are at ease
so learn balance
& be playful always
let your inner child help
what brought you energy when you were young
take out time for it
you don't have to be serious all the time
you are no god to be at your best at all times
live life through, with all its ups & down
do anything & achieve whatever you want to,
but also evolve your soul on the route
don't worry only about your physical needs
you also have to be ready
for the non-physical
do not let the shock come to you
now is the time to work through.

19
Give up

"Lowering your ego doesn't mean you're lowering your worth"

Sometimes its right to give up control,
when you don't know the zone
not everything is in your power to control
surrender to the divine,
it's the ultimate goal
you are here for a short while
so do your part well
leave else aside,
because your time is coming
there is no ultimate in this world
so your ego plays no role
these walls are mere illusion to keep yourself in control
so lower them, accept & surrender
because you will never find a place to hide from your own self,
don't create distance when it isn't needed anywhere
stop being a wall between you & your higher self
though these walls are hard to crack
but once you start the journey
you will know how to break them as well

by giving up control you will release all the energies, that meant to harm you
and will make space for good energies to come through
it's for your own good,
so you should give up when there's a need to,
because it has nothing to do with your worth
but only with your growth
because decluttering is powerful.

20
Go for it again

"Resilient, but not bitter"

Resilience is a virtue & it's commendable
not everybody has it
but that's not enough you know
though many have it,
but ask yourself, did it make you bitter? by making you work for it so much!
if it did, it wasn't worth the sacrifice.
So recognize the potential in you,
see how far you've come!
it's your quality & power that has helped you
let it make you stronger, happier, humble & wiser
not harsh, egoistic & bitter
always look at the bright side of who you are,
to build your self –worth
first discover your values & then make your own definition of success
see the bigger picture, always
my life is making me tough & ready for rejections
which is a good thing
because even I will not trust a 6 year, old with my stuff
only when you know the value
you shall get what you deserve

that's why all the tests in the world
are so tough
because not all have the strength to fight,
fail, get up & go for it again & not become bitter
because of it
these are not mere words
but the truth of life
that only when you are ready,
you shall receive
so don't get dishearten if you fail
find your resilience & go for it again
it is the ultimate test of life,
which you will have to pass, in order to
get what you want
just make sure to not lose yourself
in the flow
because your self-worth is a function
of how you value yourself throughout.

21
Grasp good

"Even the devil has qualities"

Don't choose favorites
just enjoy the game
no one is here to fail
someone today,
tomorrow else will fail
so eat your snack & enjoy the game
you've got this life to enjoy as well
so stop picking sides
because everyone has some good inside
admire the good & take it with you
in this journey of self
pick up the good even from the bad
also learn to appreciate the ones who cause you pain
because only they teach you how to stand again
there are higher & lower vibrating energies
everywhere & everyone has them
so don't get caught up in good or bad
it's the same journey of every individual here,
to transmute our lower energies into higher
frequencies
because evolution of soul only happens in the physical
body
so care only about the good,

because low vibrating energies are already high,
we do not want more
so to reach to your higher self you need to tackle them well &
these are your energies that I'm talking about
so don't look around, go within
no matter how many times you fail
but still have fun in the way
in the end,
it's in the journey in which you grasp,
all that you want to take to the top.

22
Hate

"This one is for the legends too"

Many days are such
when you hate each and everything around
when this energy accumulates,
it rises beyond control
& just a small trigger & you burst out
situations & people often do that to you
but that's fine you know
to suppress them is no option
but what's weird is
that nobody understands when you behave so off
even they go through the similar situations, but still behave like legends!
as if they have never seen this emotion before & absolutely don't know what is going on
and show absolute lack of compassion for the ones, who are going through
instead of giving space to the one who is hurting
they come and attack more
instead of understanding, they behave like fools
as if they are in some kind of contract with their beloved, that I will only understand you
and frankly, many are incapable even of that
but how small is that.

'Legends will be legends'
now,
to the one who is hurting,
when unresolved emotions accumulate, when it happens to you
try grounding,
take out time for yourself & leave all aside
this emotion doesn't define you
how you channel it, will make the world of a difference within you
it is to be channeled properly, not so you don't hurt others
but for you,
so you don't hurt yourself & let these blockages build in you
acknowledge your emotions, feel & release them like a sponge
don't let it build up in you,
because it will take all the zest of life away from you
so take some time off & sit with yourself
let whatever soothes your soul, help
walk, yoga, draw, paint, sing, listen, dance or read
create whatever you want to
do whatever help's you get still and release
& then listen to your wisdom inside
It will help you see from a higher perspective of things,
even your hate will become wise
it is better to release & even crying helps.

"If Authenticity kills you,
it's better to be dead"
-RC

Some get inspired, some get triggered
but that's exactly what's going on here

23
Head on

"You need to face your problems head on, there is no more avoiding, recognize the issue to bring the change"

Think till you exhaust & fight till you die
the most powerful spirit of the soul, is the fear of death
you cannot fight longer or survive better if you do not fear it & face it with full strength
fear death to live better,
don't only live like it's your last day
live like you own your death
because it will come sooner or later
some will go first & others later
this is a natural cycle of life
so why go unconsciously through it,
leave this body with full awareness of life
there is no escape
so whoever wants to give up on this life
listen carefully,
death won't help with that!
even death is not stronger than your karma,
so you better focus on dissolving that
so reach out to your inner self & to the high power and rise
so when there is nothing left to see in this world

then you will find your resilience there
because this is the journey of your soul
to face your fears is one way to evolve
you can't run from it,
there is no place to hide,
you will have to face it someday
so why not head on & today
rather than hiding behind our shadow self
don't let anything scare you
this is normal
it happens to us all, every now and then
no matter how strong someone looks
you don't know what they are going through or have been through
so don't let your fears define you
you're much stronger & capable than that
always tell your fears that the game is on
because you will never back-off.

24
Healing

"With seeking comes self-realization, which is key"

To heal
go within, not outside
we hold the answers to our healing
to our confidence, happiness and love
we hold the answers to everything within us
we do not need a book to read us
we have a whole book of energy within our soul
which we need to understand
find your light
which can bring you salvation
& make you whole
learn to rise from darkness & become your own hero
we do not need to look beyond ourselves for healing
we have everything we need already
let the creation, nature & your passions help you
connect to them in solitude
connect with your creativity
it has great power,
when you know how to take time out for yourself
before we look elsewhere we have to look within
but it's a habit to look elsewhere for everything
instead of finding healing, strength, happiness within
we go & look for it outside

instead of looking for love within,
we look at other people before ourselves
love will find you when you will be out there working on your goals
love will assist you in the way but it is not the final destination
so don't let love distract you, it is just there to assist you on your path
it's not bad to look for love in another
but if we haven't looked for it, within ourselves first
it's never going to feel the same.
you have to be your own healer first
and take full responsibility for your own healing,
so re-parent yourself
make yourself whole
before looking elsewhere,
look within
see which parts of you need healing
you are everything, you have everything, just see it
don't be afraid to swim through the murkiest water to bring your power back again.

25
Heartbreak

"Master the emotional realm"

You are not the only one going through it
millions before you & millions after you are going to go through this
then why do you think, you're the only special one
and your heart can never be broken
you are not the only one, love
still you distort like there is nothing else left for you to see in this world
grow up!
freedom from this attachment will come from radical acceptance
find the balance between your extremes by walking your journey
let the ice melt
let what doesn't serve you go away
let it flow & cleanse you
become the master of the emotional realm
from there will come great power
open the doors for the ones who want to go
you have the entire universe that wants your love
but only if you open your eyes to it
go serve in the charity
or go to the blind home

go do something for someone who really needs you
if nothing, just start feeding the strays outdoor
then you will realize the value that your love holds &
how much this universe really needs you
maybe the heartbreak was destined for you
so in your grief you can reach to the one who actually deserves you
or maybe it's just your karma hitting you right in the back
who knows!
but it's up to you, what you make of it
will you take the higher road or go down the same road of jealousy & drown in your own misery!
or will you do the grief work.
a whole lot of creatures & people need the love that you desire to give
so start expanding your horizons now
but if your definition of love is restricted to the intimacy alone
then how will you differentiate yourself from the rest of the animal kingdom out there?

26
Honor the re-route

"It can be a game- changer"

Honor the re-route
you're being guided to go
let things sort out by themselves, for you
because you don't know what is being handled for you
let the divine intervene
in unexpected situations that you find yourself in
they are blessings in disguise
a new way of life
so you don't have to deal with unnecessary
problems & delays
but in a choice between dealing with delays or
avoidance
wise would choose to avoid
because our eyes can't see from a higher perspective
of it
or you're being called towards your soul's call
no matter what you find yourself in
have faith
& let your worries in the flow of time
don't force the situations to happen, which are
resisting itself
switch off for a while
take another route,

it is better that way sometimes
we don't know what is being dealt for us
or something far better is waiting on the route
unfamiliar
but again, it is a personal choice
if you don't want to look either which way.
sometimes when we don't leave the things that are
not meant for us
and we don't answer our soul's call
we might struggle & get it any way
but then something else will be taken away from us
just to restore the balance
which would have been more fulfilling for your
emotional & physical growth
but you will never know
unless you choose to take risk & the route you're
being guided to go
if something is not happening for you, don't lose hope,
it means it's time to learn patience, that's all
it can be a game-changer for you.

27
Humans

"Learn to co-exist"

Remove your false glasses of ego
this world is not yours alone
it will survive even if you die
so it's not somehow your birth right to control
divinity & creatures beyond your limited knowledge exist
look beyond your walls
there is a lot more you don't realize
human laws are not the only one's protecting us
it's the nature's acceptance of our existence & behavior which is protecting us
thankfully the universe is not in our control
otherwise it would end up dead in 1 day alone
it's always us, who ask the universe to give something to us
but the real question is, what have you given it back, what energy have you put out
you think you will give out hurt & hate in the world & receive love from the universe?
you're so delusional
even the devotion & faith have just become mere tools, so your life can become comfortable & you can get more, that's all

& the energy behind it is not coming from the place of pure love for this nature or the universe
and still,
even if you're being selfish, this universe will love you back
so don't feel betrayed when your hard work doesn't pay
because that's the only concern these days,
not the internal satisfaction but the final fruition we claim
however,
have faith,
the fruits will still come back to you in some way
but it's your power to recognize what has been given to you, when you least expect.

28
Invest within

"You are the best thing that has happened to you"

You will have it
to feel free & absolute
it's time to invest within
you have to be the magician
so you can create whatever you want
be your authentic self,
be your eccentric self, first
tap into your visionary,
into your expansive
know your uniqueness
so you can create that, what you want for yourself
the world is your playground
but first gather strength
so you don't collapse on the very first day
you are your most valuable asset
so do the work within
instead of being torn
get immersed inwards till the outside world is
completely gone
in stillness, it will come to you.
strength doesn't rely on the muscles
it comes from the spirit
it's about the trust,
that the universe has your back
so find balance within to disconnect & to reconnect
you are worthy of your investment.

29
Karma

"Truth cannot be taught. It's realized"

Keep your energy high
by not holding a grudge against any situation,
things might not have worked out in the past or may have gone wrong
or someone really hurt you throughout the years
maybe they lied to you or did you wrong
but it's important to find forgiveness within,
for those who hurt you, but not for them at all
but for you, to free yourself from the slavery of your emotions
because only when you forgive
will their karmic cycle begin;
let the universe take control
because only when you will truly end the cycle in which you are,
the karma will do her payout
so break free, by forgiving
and no holding on to the hurt & lies
or what they did or didn't do to you in the past or now,
holding onto those energies will only create a block in you like a huge brick wall, building one by one
& you can't even look over it anymore

it's blocking your blessings,
your beliefs & your trust in the good
so forgive & then leave it be
wait no more.
you don't have to ask for them to suffer
be the bigger person,
focus every bit of your energy on you
the ones who make others suffer
will absolutely suffer, one way or another
karma always gets back, it spares no one
because it's a mirror
but you should not ask for it,
be wise & humble always
those who harm will pay back
& if you choose to give out love you will receive it back
so those who choose bad, they can't be stopped
because even they have a free will to do so
it's their choice to create another karmic loop for themselves,
but you forgive & focus on dissolving your karma till then
good will come your way so work with pure intentions & energy for it
it's with the universe's permission that we exist,
so no one is smart enough to fool or just pass it by.
the count is kept & the debt has to be paid
it just works like a bank, with interest depending upon the amount you took.

30
Level up

"Learn how to be here & be alive, by faith, grounding & inner silence"

Level up your game
it isn't a fairy tale
come back to reality
when time numbs the pain
it's okay to take time off
but not to get stuck
you are power yourself
life is harsh,
but good too will come
it's on you to see it such
you will need no helping hand
if you have trust within yourself
this time will end too
just be graceful till then
don't fall down into the arms of others
learn to get up when you fall on the ground
it's okay to cry & it's fine to scream
learn to handle yourself & become strong within
only then will come the strength, to stand again
because this is life and you will fall again
how many times will others help?

31
Lion

"Choose a mission that is bigger than yourself"

Know how to express your power
be the lion that you are
he is not taught to stand in his power
he knows how to take over
he knows it in his blood
a lion doesn't roar to ask for permission
he roars to demand that I am here in my power
so build strength because it doesn't come in a go
but it is there if you look for,
for all the right reasons
balance your power in a healthy way
so anger doesn't step in
discover your unique strengths
so you lead your life in a whole
be fearless while expressing your power
& never follow the ones who abuse their,
work on yourself,
so you don't turn out the same way
you are being called to the next level
to step up into the leadership role
for yourself
so you can be loyal to your truth & embody your
strength

and make a stand
be the lion that you are,
don't stand behind your shadow self, if you don't like something,
cut it away
don't complaint & talk this or that
never lower yourself
don't give away your power to anything
so nothing can shake you, as it like
assert yourself in a healthy way
for your betterment & manifesting the best
channel your energies in the right way.

32
Love

"Don't restrict such a beautiful emotion only for one"

Love is ultimate
then why not love all
deeper your inner love & find love in everything around
why restrict it to one & then ask for it in return
why distort when one's love is denied
personal relationships are important, we know
but why to make our whole life about them
they are just a part of our life, not our whole life
so to restrict such a pure feeling only for our own is not justified
how do you become the bigger person then?
anyone in this world can love their own
the true power lies when you can show love even to those whom you don't like
& the ones who really need
if someone dear leaves,
be it death, misunderstanding or cheating
there is no need to be in chaos & pain
it was just a phase you signed up for before coming here
it sounds harsh, but

they taught you the lesson & now it's time for you to move forward & evolve
It is a painful loss,
but you can't be in that energy for your whole life long
do take time off,
but don't stop living your life, there is still a lot left to unravel
evolve your emotional body & master your emotions
grow beyond this physical love that the movies taught
break free from the matrix programming
love is most pure, deep & an unconditional emotion
which means without condition
so love the whole world,
every creature, the river, the rock, the divine & even your neighbors
don't restrict such a beautiful emotion just for one
the whole world is meant to be loved.

33
Medicine

"It can be your karmic kick as well"

When you think you've done nothing wrong
when something bad happens to you
just accept and surrender at that time
accept reality and come out of the fool's paradise
it's the judgment time
it's your karma giving your medicine back to you
it's not always the other's fault
for what we are going through
we can only recall a few years &
say we did nothing wrong to get this
but you have no clue
what wrong deeds & energies have you put out
someone you hurt,
chose to do wrong to or
didn't learn the lesson, when you were meant to,
even if something happened in your favor earlier
you didn't evolve from what life was trying to teach you
so the life is giving you another lesson again
there are many reasons for what everyone goes through
not everyone goes to the human prison for the crime they commit

it is the supreme court of energy
which knows how to balance each and everything out,
without your validation
it is above all
a war that you can never win
consciously or unconsciously done
but what's done is done
there is no reversal to it
we can forget the count
but karma keeps account
apologizing only makes the room for acceptance to come, in order to accept your lesson now
because that's how you evolve,
so you can finish this cycle once & for all
but you will surely get back what you have given out
there is no escape from karma
but if you have good intentions & acceptance
you can break free from it
by accepting & learning your lessons well
me, you & everyone will get it
so think again before you wrong anyone else
karma will surely come around
what you are giving to the world
exactly that will be given back to you
karma coming around is no joke
it will hurt really bad
sooner or later you will surely know
one way or another
either love or trouble,

be ready for whatever energy you have put out
if anything goes wrong,
just accept it the way it happened to you & don't be resentful
and avoid getting into another karmic loop
because life will keep putting you through the same situations till you learn your lessons well & become humble as well
and death can't help you in any which way
it's just an illusion
because your karma status will not change,
and you will have to go through the same life cycles all over again
death is just a journey from bondage of physical to the freedom of the non-physical
without any changes in your karma, till you dissolve it
so start seeking your liberation
& move through this life with full awareness
so you can live and die well.

34
Mental freedom

"Master the mental realm"

Self-validate,
don't find your self -worth in others
move beyond the constraints of mind
if you believe, it will happen
you have the freedom to step out of the box,
to do it differently
be careful of the negative thought patterns
that come to you
or you will unconsciously manifest them for you
if something is happening unconsciously doesn't mean it is not happening
so be aware of every thought that comes to your mind
it takes an immense amount of energy,
so put it to use
but don't let your own mind trick you
overpower & release the negative
acknowledge where they are coming from
it is tough, because we can't see objectively if it's happening inside of our head
it takes a lot of awareness overtime
which takes a long time
to absorb these messages

even the most open minded people need a lot of time to work through this
so don't hide or drown in them
they often come & it's not easy
but in order to get better you have to manifest better
& it happens from within
so don't hurt yourself unconsciously
don't be trapped in your own cage
release yourself
it is possible to be free
get back in control of your system
make your mind work for you
understand all its tricks & treats
so you don't tempt into buying any
get in control of your imaginations,
for fear, to leave your life!
& master the mental realm
and your whole world will change
start seeing things from all perspectives
without any emotional hindrance to it
you will start getting better at it, by becoming rational
& more conscious of it
by keeping your ego and pride away.
lightening is needed to destroy the old,
so you can rebuild & sunny sky can come through
don't get caught up in the mental cycles
you don't want to see yourself in
let your higher self in this physical vessel
& become free of the negative patterns
so you can always look from the higher perspective of things.

35
Mess

"Let it make you wise"

When a mess,
surrender to not knowing
leave the questions alone which are beyond the ordinary
it may seem like,
there is no way to go
but let the storm pass
it's better to lay low,
than to fight it alone
time will change, it will heal all wounds
so just go through the pain,
that's the only way to grow
don't run away from it,
it hurts because it's supposed to
growing is not easy, ask the seed you sowed
even through all the seasons,
its growing, though alone
a day will come when you will bear the fruit
just devote yourself for your higher good
so don't overdo, its fine & your time will change soon
it's not for everyone to know
just the ones who seek to grow

till then, you need to keep a high vibrating energy
physically, mentally & energetically
so try grounding &
and let even the mess in your life make you wise.

Your energy comes first, everything else is secondary

you can help others, if you help yourself first

so fill your own cup before pouring into others.

36
No one is here for you

"The one who wants others to prove, so you can decide if you should too, come out of this illusion, they are not here for you"

Let go off the wells that are poisoned to drink from
it is not water in them anymore
bow down for the time it served you
and move on
there is no sense to stand & cry over it
seasons will change
and happiness will restore
so start seeing life from a different lens now
the way forward goes step by step
lay down your burdens first
little by little you will understand
if you're joyful,
everything is beautiful
it's the beauty in you that sees the beauty around
& the consciousness that sees the details in all
so start seeing the world with your naked eyes
there are dimensions which exist beyond you & I
so start evolving now
every answer cannot be served in the silver spoon to you
so start seeking for yourself now

lower your walls of opinions & become receptive to the knowledge, so you can go beyond
nobody has incarnated here to prove anything to you or specially for you
everybody is here for their own journey & growth
so stop giving so much importance to yourself now,
that only if someone gives me proof will I do.
it's easy to live & die unaware,
but awareness will need work
if it were that easy
then what are we still doing here
the entire world should have liberated by now
& if you don't care
that's totally fine
it's your journey not mine
one can only tell
& rest is up to you
some learn the hard way,
but it doesn't have to be you.

37
Opinions

"I will only & I will never, are bold statements, which limit you & procrastinate your soul's call due to your free will"

Opinions will limit,
but seeking will grow
see life, as it is for
no one is alike outside
so embrace the difference even if you don't like
stop caring what one's wearing
rather widen your mind &
change your perspective
because every soul is alike
they have chosen their & you have chosen your right
see the bigger picture every time
find the path which fulfills your life,
rather than to criticize
these are petty things, which will only boost ego
but nothing meaningful in life
one remains superficial & will never understand the depth of life
and there's no purpose for an insignificant life
so lower your walls of opinions
and start seeking now
become receptive, if you want to know more,
even if you read all the books in the world,

there will still be somethings that will be left out
so grow everyday
than to limit yourself
there is a lot more still to know
because as wise as you become the more frictionless
this life will turn out for you.

38
Overpower

"To take your power back is also an art, not instantly always but within time"

If accidently,
you gave your power to someone
learn to take it back
even if you have to go through a period of isolation
which is actually good
but that's the biggest fear these days
to feel left out
anyways!
accept everything as it comes to you
bad or worse
to lose hope is no option
take a stand if you can
call out the crap, with dignity
but if the situation is such
choose acceptance
believe in time & the universe
if you are really true
time will give your power back to you
gather your strength & accept
know, when to take the silent road
it's not possible to give it back every time
so wait for the right time

acceptance is a choice that only you can make
don't fall apart in that time
that's the moment to show your grace
take the fall if you have to, but with integrity intact within
take its power back from over you
focus on the solution then,
& if there is none
let the time fix it for you
it does & it will
so focus on yourself
it's just a matter of time
it always gets better
no matter the situation
but time only intervenes,
if you don't take the judgment in your hands
because when time takes control, one dies of thirst in the water
with all the money & food, one will not be able to eat
that's how time takes play
now you see, what is it that you want
if you want to take control & get in another loop of life
or let the time take over for you
because it spares no one, not even you
however powerful you think you or they are.

Personal gratification over spirituality

39
Playfulness

"Tap into your inner child & take a playful approach"

With self- awareness,
shift you fear based consciousness into the vibration of love
our physical expression is what we are feeling inside,
so tap into the power of joy,
the sacredness within you
strip yourself from what keeps you down
you are no god walking on this earth
you don't have to be serious all the time
be witty & play full
do things, that connect you to the child in you
the collective has lost its innocence, but don't let it defeat you
what was that, that brought fun to you when you were young?
which is that one thing, that brought you the energy to make you feel fully alive & made you forget the outside world completely
connect to that energy now
don't let only fear teach you how to be alive,
there are better ways too,
like tapping into your inner child
what was it,

while doing, you didn't look at the time
connect with that passion in you
however silly you think it might look
work from that & start playing a little
life doesn't have to be so serious
if you tap into that energy, even spirituality is fun
instead of following others,
create your own path
let your inner child out
you can have fun on every path that you wish to walk
rephrase your energies,
you don't have to be working under stress
it is not written anywhere
that only stress will bring you your success
if you play
you release
you are vibrant & happy
then every day becomes a success
you will not have to wait to achieve something to make you happy
you will be happy everyday
ups & downs will still come
but the child energy will help you overcome
take the playful approach at all times
it will ease down your life.

40
Rainbow

"Don't close your eyes just before time"

The rainbow doesn't come
before the rain,
so stop resisting the change
after the rain, move ahead
by releasing the rest
the road hasn't been easy, I know
but the difficult part is over or will be over soon
learn to acknowledge that as well,
when it's time to heal!
for the time you are here,
make full use of it
let your pain guide you & others who come your way
channelize your pain into your power &
become a rainbow for yourself & all the eyes that see
don't let the pain take away, the joy in you
it comes natural & is comfortable
but don't let the toxicity get to you
step out of your comfort zone
it's that moment which decides, that do you have the
power in you?
don't let your pain trap you,
to go in your shell & become sad are the easiest route,
so take the difficult route,

even if tears come with you
never close off that beautiful heart in you
express your emotions in such a way
that they come out of you as a rainbow for everyone who sees you
find your light while pain is happening to you
so you don't close yourself to the new
that's the time to take over control
learn to heal yourself, on your own
why to give someone else the strength to come & heal us
don't depend, but become strong in that moment
& be there for yourself,
with time accept the good when it comes your way
& never be afraid
it has happened to each & every one of us someday
so learn to make the best out of your pain as well.

41
Reality check

"Learn to relax in the present"

Let down your umbrella
that you think, is protecting you from rain
but what you don't see is, that it is also keeping you from cleansing
so let it down
surrender & let the divine come into play
let the rain water cleanse your body & soul
drop the illusion that only you know what is working best for you
because the bad in your mind in real is protecting you
let the divine timing course through
what we think is best for ourselves is not actually true
so don't let your illusions enslave you
stop forcing things to happen, they are already happening for you
the way they are falling into place for you, you require a higher perspective to understand that
there is a power beyond you & I which we can't control
not everything is black & white
there is another fine line
you need your third eye to realize
self-realization is the ultimate key

so resist the impulse to go ahead with your first instinct,

take time to tune into your deeper intuition

power is born in that time when you relax in the present moment.

Merkaba – Sacred geometry

42
Refuse

"Let your soul choose"

Refuse to do that,
that doesn't make you happy or fulfil your soul's call
don't do anything that doesn't serve you emotionally,
step into your truth
what is meant to be, will surely enter your life
so don't struggle unnecessarily
but you need to reciprocate your energy to receive it by
you have to make space in your vessel for the right energies you want to attract
so refuse, empty & cleanse your vessel first
and it takes time, a lot of it
so refuse everything that strays you from your path,
it's tough at the beginning, it really is
but only then you will be truly ready to receive,
once you've done the work
and you know your worth
you will automatically not accept anything less than, what doesn't work,
you will know, what is right & when is the right time
if your soul decides
so let your inner wisdom speak to you in stillness
whenever you are stuck in between choices

you are worthy
let time speak for yourself
just put in the work in the right directions till then
but always choose to do what aligns you with your higher self
because there is no situation that cannot rise itself again
it's a cycle which you have to break
that's why you are being brought to the same situations over & over again
to get to the college
you will have to pass your school first
because a school kid will not know, what to do with the college books
so you need to complete schooling first
whether you like it or not
so you can bring your understanding
to that level of consciousness
where life becomes frictionless for you.

43
Respect

"Respect is claimed within, there is no need to look for it anywhere else"

If you look for respect outside
it will never be enough
it is only appropriate if you have it for yourself
then even if someone doesn't
it will never bother you
because how someone behaves,
speak for themselves
not for you,
your respect is not someone's opinion
that they can give
it is a feeling one should have within
only if you acknowledge it in you, will you be able to acknowledge it in others
understanding starts from within
if you don't know who you are, what your powers & boundaries are
then you will easily give them away
so do right by you
without harming any
even when no one is looking, your higher self is
develop integrity & values in you
no one is born with it

but what you learn & decide to acquire speaks for you
step into your power
observe your patterns & learn yourself better
then respect for oneself comes automatically
it's an internal process
to understand others, start with yourself first
because what is given to you,
can also be taken away
so why to give anyone that power
which is truly yours to claim
so learn to drive your own car & not depend on others
to take you in the right direction always.

44
Rest up

"Don't be too hard on yourself"

Rest up when you feel drained
when you feel like nothing is working your way
because this is the time
when your patience most counts
leave it all be & rest up for a while
take time to get back on your feet
because it's just a matter of time
& then things will turn around for you, when you will least expect
so don't lose it till then
because that counts
don't waste your energies everywhere
learn to walk away from things
not every fight is yours to fight
when you have the ability to choose your fights
only stand when its right to,
else its wasting your energy & time
calm yourself down
eat your favorite food & relax
gain your strength back in that time,
leave all worries for a while
because life will still happen, even if you are not alive
so stop taking all the burden on your shoulders
it's okay to rest up every once in a while

45
Set boundaries

"Be selective & set firm boundaries"

Set physical & energetic boundaries
know your boundaries even in the limitless zone
reach the frequency where you need no laws to co-exist
but sense & telepathy
as high as our frequency rises,
the closer we get to the divine
it's not a one-way route
open your channels & let the divine come half way to you
there is magic in nature,
there is love
so believe
do the inner work so you can vibrate higher!
and rise your energies to tap into the infinite potential within you
with patience & pure intentions
soon you will counter your higher self
so grow beyond & devote your soul for the higher good
let your experiences make you wise,
not traumatized.
there is no final test after which you graduate

it's an ongoing process
because change is the only constant
and you can never be done with life here
but it will help you change your perspective
let tests & temptations come your way
it's up to you to not settle right there,
as soon as it looks comfortable
in order to reach your destiny
be with all, but detached to all
know when to walk away or to stay
earn money but don't revolve around it
set your boundaries straight
know, who & what to allow in your personal space
be selective of who should enter your sacred space
hold your boundaries for good & let no one overstep them
be it physical, material, emotional or energetic boundaries
there is a higher purpose for everyone here
make the needed boundaries with the external, so you can align with your higher self
that's where the ultimate ecstasy lies
be in a state of total reverence for all things
but to hold your boundaries & maintaining it is must
so you can balance your energies well.

46
Solitude

"Rephrase your reality, learn to be comfortable both in partnership & in solitude"

A person with integrity
is not afraid of the journey
it's time to level up
to balance your energy
to move in a new direction
to transcend patterns & behaviors
that no longer serve you
it's time to move forward
to become your own boss
perceive your struggles in a positive way to re-write your past
to grow & transform
you can start fresh today
awaken to the awareness of your own potential
if you believe, it will happen
rephrase your reality
shift your energies
you need no body's validation
let them misunderstand you & let them reject
not everyone can match your frequency
block the loud noise coming from outside & anchor wisdom and love in you

by realizing how life happens & why things happen
you will know better
so you can break the chains,
overcome your wounds & traumas
& see your dark in a new light
surrender your belief in scarcity
all is possible
it is time to go within
to connect to your subconscious & answer your soul's calling
solitude will help
you can only hear yourself when you stop hearing everything else from your energy field & the physical realm
now take time off for rejuvenating yourself
just like 769
one step forward
take another back
take time off, replenish & then go for it
two times strong
learn how to balance work & play
embrace solitude & stand in your own power always.

47
Solution

"Always come up with solutions & put every soul at ease around you"

Anyone can tell
what the problem is,
only a few who can really point out
the solutions for it
integrate solutions in yourself, then pointing out mistakes in everything around
become a solution for everything &
bring your focus on fixing
evolve your soul by working
through it
& do not get stuck at the question
you are not here to waste life or just let it pass by
you are here for more
you are here for growth
put every soul & thing at ease around you
bring that much balance in you
that you become a magnet for all the good energies to come to you
all have enough problems of their own
try to bring solutions to those places & areas which need you
create a space for all to exist in harmony

become someone who lightens up the room
who brings peace in a fight
but also be appreciative, if someone else does that for you
become the bigger person in every situation
that is presented to you,
let others also see the light in you
so even they can be aware,
that there is a better way to do little things in everyday life too
choose tranquility above all.

48
Spiritual hunger

"The feeling of emptiness arises, when we confuse our basic requirements with luxury"

Why do you feel empty inside?
even when you have it all
why are you drained out?
where is this feeling coming from?
why are you in a consistent cycle of negative thoughts?
what exactly is your soul asking for?
is it a physical hunger, material hunger, food or spiritual hunger, that your body is craving for!
what is it, have you ever figured it out?
because of the number of choices that we have
we often confuse our wants with our needs
just like our body needs water but we want juice
then no matter how much juice you consume, it will never be enough & won't do the job
because the basic need of the body has not been met
you will always be thirsty
the basic requirement can never be replaced even by a healthy drink
for survival you only require water
there is no life without it
but you can definitely survive without a glass of juice

the same goes for our soul
so ask the right questions to yourself,
that is the first step,
so you can start seeking the right answers
because our soul needs nourishment too
you need to satisfy the spirits needs first
so you can feel content within
without looking anywhere else for it.
energy is the soul's fuel
you need to balance that which is greater than you
so you can fulfil your spirit's basic needs.
In this modern world
we are confusing our basic needs with luxury,
which is not correct
just because you're busy & don't have time to look
within or sit with yourself & ask the right questions
doesn't mean you are the ultimate one
just because you have a lot more to distract you
doesn't mean your soul's requirement is fulfilled
so look within
because we only have a few years left to do the work
we came here for
and as it is, it is a personal choice for all of you.

49
Spiritual life

"Spirituality is not a place that hides you or asks you to leave anything aside, to pursue it"
it simplifies & liberates.

For the ones who are unaware,
to be spiritual,
doesn't mean you get to hide or run from the world,
when the world isn't serving you right or
leaving all your duties aside
it can also be lead, while fulfilling all your responsibilities here
it comes from 'self- realization'
it is to be lead the same way you maintain your professional & domestic life
now the time is to inculcate spiritual life as well
hurt, pain or loss of a beloved
usually triggers that in many
but after the trigger has done its job
you can't keep working from that place
be it fear or pain
spiritual life will never ask you to leave your physical or material wealth
it is that when the awakening happens inside of you
and 'self-realization' comes into play

you automatically detach from everything that is external to you
without anyone asking you to do it
now when you have reached that point
it is one's personal choice, of what they want to leave behind
some go into the absolute
others decide to consciously pursue
but that point cannot be reached without "self - realization" first
many can help you follow & many follow religiously
but enlightenment can only come from within
no one can do the job for you
just like no one can digest the food you eat for you
one can only teach or instruct & they are doing a wonderful job for you
but following instructions is not enough
you need to seek yourself too
the whole point of 'self-realization is that, only you can do it for you,
with the help of the spiritual teachers that are there to guide you
to feel content & blissful is rare these days
for the ones who think,
that who could not make anything of their life goes for it,
they are the most delusional type
they take life the most casually
as they have a lot more to distract them and keep them busy

but what's there to understand is
the people with single plate of food do not throw it away
they know the value of it
but the ones who have so many choices to eat,
waste it
it has many meanings you can go with it however you like
to take the path of liberation or not is your personal choice.

50
Surrender

"Surrender to the divine, whomever you see that pure energy in"

Let go off control & surrender,
believe in somethings
even if you don't see them coming
it's the battle of patience in your downfall
until you rise again
many give up too soon
but that's all that counts,
that who will stand
when the worst is around & only those shall pass the test of soul
who shall not give up.
now for the pain,
let the destiny play its role
because no matter how ready you are
there is still much to figure out
there is much more depth
than you see to it
so leave it all alone & reflect on yourself
self -control & solitude will teach you strength
let things come to you & be patient till then
meanwhile find your inner strength
surrender yourself & all your problems to the divine

if you're here, you're totally capable of being here on your own,
but there is no need to go through this life & your problems alone
so give it all away & share it with the divine
it will accept you just for who you are
with no judgments for what you have done
just devote yourself to the high power & keep on moving through this life
only if you put that pure intensity of energy into something
you will see the power behind.

51
Temperance

"Balance fire & water with a rainbow"

I am no king or queen
but I hold the energies of the masculine & the feminine
I walk with both inside &
I walk with grace
I can fight,
nurture as well
I understand
& also make mistakes
but I accept with compassion even if its late
I love water, but I am made of fire
I am pure myself, but I am the ruler of impurities
I am wise
& impulsive too
but I devote myself for my highest good
I look as modern as the time
but I am an old soul of ancient times
who balances her fire & water energies with a rainbow,
I can destroy like fire & give life like water
but I balance myself with pure intentions & compassion
there is no more need to prove anything

I know myself & that's enough for me
I can burn for what's right & also flow away when it's right
I can fight the strongest and apologize from the weakest
and that's where my true power lies
I understand that even through the mud my soul can come out clean & nothing more, that I see
I distance myself from the bad energies
because I am scared to unleash me,
fire in me is uncontrollable, if I like it to be
so I like to flow away like the river sometimes
so I don't get caught up in my own heat
because even after winning that fight,
my feminine will bleed with compassion & humility inside
so why should I bring myself to that!
nothing scares me, but I still like to get scared at times
so I can balance my energies with love & compassion at all times
because if I lose it! my own humility stares at me
so balance, that's my way of life.

Triple moon goddess *Horned god*

The masculine & the feminine energy

together they make equal & opposite in gender polarity.

52
The Alchemy

"Learn to transmute energies, so everything you touch turns to gold" & even the negative benefits you positively"

We are the conduits of energy
so focus on your channel
let the evolution happen in you
we have the potential within, to transmute our lower vibrations into higher frequencies
that is another step towards the journey of self
& that's what we are here for
self-absorbed people & situations are only here to fuel you
don't take anything personal
but always decide to grow
if you decide to take the better way
everything will change
because you & your fate is just one decision away
if you can change your energies
your whole life path can change
but it is not an easy job
it is not as easy as it is said
once you work on them
your decision will be tested again & again
till the point you break
but still if you keep standing by your decision

then the time will turn in your favor
if you want to reach somewhere your power has to be tested first
like, just according to the rank you're given a government seat
In order to reach where you are meant to be
you need to work without the safety net
so you can take a leap with your whole force
have faith in you & time itself
so you can develop power with integrity
otherwise you can see many misusing their powers
but they will pay
no one can be stopped from the decision they are taking
as the divine never interferes with free will
everyone has their freedom to choose,
which will define them
in either which way they would like to
& accordingly you will get back what you sow
the trigger energies are here
so we can align with are higher self or lower
whichever path, one wants to go
it's your decision alone.

53
The Fuel

"Know the energy which fuels your intention"

If you've come this far, that you chose to align with your higher self
it is commendable
but,
now that, you've chosen the right path,
took the right decision & taking the right steps towards it
it doesn't stop at that
it is to know that
the job will still not be done
because it doesn't work that way
if it were that easy, there was no need for seeking
& many would have achieved nirvana by now
what is there to know is that
the main thing is the intention & the energy behind taking any decision whether good or bad
be it, the best thing for you, all humanity or even the universe
however good the deed is
but what is the energy behind that, you are working from
that is the real deal
we are all energies here in the physical vessel

so it can help us evolve to a higher dimension
is it out of fear or pride,
that we are choosing to do right?
look within, ask,
is it the ego playing behind the scene?
where is it coming from?
is the energy that is fueling the intention, coming from the place of pure love & devotion!
or just so you can be seen right
because if it is so,
it's not going to work for you.
maybe,
you may have chosen the higher road
because of some pain or suffering that you experienced
maybe through some emotion,
but understand
that, that's exactly the triggers job
so you can align with your highest self
but after the alignment has happened
you can't keep working from that space
after you understand that
working for your higher good
needs to come from the purest of intentions in your heart
even the unconscious intention & energies should be right
because only then the devotion is pure
you can hide from anybody in the world
but you can't hide from your soul & the universe

so whatever you chose, work on the energy behind
only then it will work for you
take instructions from the right people
but never stop seeking & evolving within
if you truly want to be enlightened
it will never come from following
one can only tell you,
which is the right way to go,
but seeking
it should come from within
for surrendering to the ultimate
your energy behind the decision
should also be ultimate
it should only come out from the place of love,
wisdom & compassion,
gratitude and humbleness
without any intentions of harming any
can you ask for love from above!

54
The Magician

"As above so below, also forms a star, become the creator of your reality"

You are a star
for you anything is possible,
but everything is optional
just ask for what you want!
you are the magician
so go within as without
deepen your roots
so no one can touch your grounds
but accept the fate
when your branches break
strong roots will help them grow again
have gratitude for the time it spent
learn your lesson & let it go away
this is the cycle of life
the one who breaks, will grow again from within you or without
but if you want to grow again!
ground yourself & strengthen your roots within,
learn to create
see everything as a phase which will someday end
enjoy the phase till it lasts again
because it is going to end one day

no matter how hard you try to hold on, it will slip away like sand
so live now, right now
& make the most of it
as it will not remain the same for very long
but don't become a mess when you break
it will hurt
but believe that time will change,
so till then
learn & heal yourself
so you can rejuvenate & bear the fruits when the season change
you are your own star
let your healing come from within
shine your light even in the darkest night
so not only you, but even others can see their way through your light
you have the power to build whatever you want for yourself in this life
so don't cry when something breaks,
you only evolve from every situation, problem & mistake,
you can tap into the energy of the magician & create all that you want for yourself
grow from every phase that you are exposed to,
you gain from each & everything
just evolve, from all of it
there should be no staying stagnant for you
then you charge forward with all that you have got in you

channel them into your passion
and go for it with full strength
then you will see how things work out for you
themselves.

I
THE MAGICIAN.

55
The Past

"It's time to move forward, you have already dragged it beyond its expiration date"

Be it good, bad, traumatic, amazing or not
there is no point & validation for dwelling on
what happened, is already done
there is no point in waking the dead
in the amidst of life
don't let the pressure here & there deter you
learn to handle pressure
what you have is right now
don't let the past situations hold you back
from what you're capable off
no one has the power to define you
be your haters or even loved ones
only you know who you are, what life experiences have you been through
so again
no one & absolutely no one has the right to tell you
who you are & what you're meant to do
don't listen to those who don't even know themselves yet
who have no clue of their own existence here!
because a wise person will never do that
these thought patterns when they come again

make sure to gather & release them
acknowledge & feel, but let them go
don't let your emotions make you work for them
even if it was traumatic you can choose to become wise
don't let it take the best of you
let your light guide you
the one who wants to grow can change overnight too
so don't let anyone prick you
you have the time today to start new
& let them bugger off who come to deter you
they are all souls around you
no matter how close or far they are
you & everyone in your life has signed a contract to come in this form here
to meet you in this life time,
so nobody is doing anyone a favor
they accepted to come in form of your parents & you accepted the position of their child
just like that goes for every relation you will ever have
you have to respect everyone but never lose yourself for anyone
everyone is here for their own journey.
so never limit yourself from your or their opinions
why only past
free yourself from what others think too
they have their dark sides too
which they don't want anyone to know
but if you behave the same way they do

they will have no place to run from you
but never disgrace yourself like that
dignity is not it, if you forget
so see beyond what your eyes really show
let all your experiences teach you & grow.

56
Torch

"Let your intuition come into play"

Navigate through illusions
awaken your dormant energies
experience from other senses as well
taste, smell & embrace your sensuality as well
it is not always the heart and mind that should be in control
let your intuition guide as well
let it be the torch when nothing else works
strengthen your bond with it
make energetic upgrade
integrate it, in yourself
so you can follow your own sense,
where to go or not to.
take charge of who you are
your intuitions can guide you well,
if you get in tune with them
other senses will play a vital role
but for them to take over
open your channel first
your feelings are very true
develop them
so when you can't see
your feelings will still keep on helping you

there is more potential in you, than just to see or hear
so activate your other senses,
start feeling life than just seeing it
then there can be nothing that blocks you
your possibility for more will increase
step up your game
see the potential in you & this life
be the torch for yourself
so if your batteries die
you will still have backup in you to prevail
let your other senses work like the generator
on which you can always rely
but only if you fuel it beforehand.

57
Triggers

"Don't let the triggers trick you into ego"

Triggers are here to align you with what you came here to do
it's time to think from a higher perspective
bow down to the one who sparked that fire in you
but now as you align
don't let it come from a place of ego
there is no need for you to prove anyone
let it come from your highest self
let your wisdom speak through your consciousness
it's just the nature's way to bring you to what you are meant to
it won't come and say directly to you
it's for you to understand
it is a way to push you to the edge
then let your actions speak for yourself
there is no need for revenge
whatever you do is for you
to align you with your highest self
not so you work from your ego
there is no need to belittle the one who triggered you
be it, a person or a situation
always have gratitude
for whoever served you, in the right direction

sometimes love is not enough
so you are given tough love
so you can learn your lessons firsthand
and start working on them when it is time for you to move ahead
but remember,
the universe never interferes with free will
you have the freedom to choose what you want to do
you will never be stopped from doing that
but whatever you choose to give out
your karma will surely give it all back to you
so never lose your humbleness,
no matter how high you rise.
also,
always remember to speak your truth,
maybe you are the trigger for some other soul here,
so it can align with its higher self
so never hold resentment for anybody
you will never know what job of the universe are you doing unconsciously.

Triumph of spirit over matter & earthly desire

58
Walk away

"Walk away if it's your self- respect at stake"

Away you go
when you don't feel right
your intuition will guide
walk the path of thorns for no ego but self
respect alone
there is a higher purpose
an end beyond you & I
which we will not know
until we reach it so
so walk away from what doesn't serve you right
there is another road which is still unidentified
you will reach,
where you are meant to be
so don't hold onto things which consume your light
so when its dark you can shine
at the end of the tunnel you will find your right,
but not what you felt was right.
so don't settle for less
because only walking away will bring you to your
best.

59
Wealth

"Dismantle the unconscious programming & manifest universe's love for yourself"

Wealth is the ultimate goal
for comfort, revenge, happiness & to show others your success
it is not your fault that you think this way
that only with money comes power
as it has been programmed into you a certain way, at the subconscious level
it is not bad for wanting to be comfortable
but in the process don't forget your roots
for what are we really here for?
evolution of soul only happens in the physical realm
so even if you desire comfort
do not make your whole life about it
come into simple ways of being
& to not live in the material way of thinking
go work hard, achieve
but never stop working on yourself
the real power comes from within
it builds in you overtime,
your experiences will make you wise
what happens in internal is the ultimate reality of external

and if it isn't,
it is better not to hide
don't start & end your day around money,
physical things are mere distractions
the ultimate goal is your soul's liberation
so keep working on that
don't attach yourself to wealth
work for it, but be detached
find happiness within
by working on yourself
with integrity, simplicity, seeking & acceptance
with gratitude & humbleness,
manifest the universe's love for yourself
don't get stuck on wealth, see beyond that
what is ahead?
now when we have reached a certain stage
it is our responsibility to become aware
so we can dismantle the wrong programming in our head
so start going within
gather that intensity of energy
so you can live & die consciously
even if it comes early.

60
Why?

"You can't be stagnant & just pass by"

The unstable mind doesn't easily go into the meditative zone
the thoughts that you run from,
in stillness, come through first
it is not an easy task to just go from nothing to all
start by taking a step forward & not jump
start by relaxing so you can be your own healer,
understand & contemplate
why something happened to you, there is always a reason
there is no such thing as coincidence in life lessons
you are just where you are meant to be
so sooth your mind first
do what will relax you
go sing, write or dance maybc cook
whatever let your tears out
release the first wall of trauma, hate, loss, ego, fear, guilt or shame
go into the silent zone & acknowledge what is going on
understand what is hurting you so much & look beyond
in that zone do not lie to yourself

as humans are even capable of that

be true to oneself & accept what happened to you and what you are supposed to learn from that

without blaming yourself or anyone involved

why that situation happened to you, you need to make yourself understand

was it to teach or trigger you

or for your higher good!

to make you strong or make you release whatever was inside of you

there are many reasons to why something has happened to you

but that's why we are here

so learn & evolve

& only the dark will help you find your light

trust that the time will heal all wounds

and it will pass

but grasp what is life trying to teach you, from that very experience itself

you don't want the same situation coming again

because it will happen again, till you do not learn what your meant to

so think from a higher perspective

we are not here to just graduate from school or college life alone

life lessons are taught by time

you evolve or don't is up to you

maybe the little problem was to save you from a bigger disaster,

start looking within for answers

now close your eyes & let your inner eyes see, what your wide open eyes missed

& release all your pain & worries in time

you are never alone love

the higher realms are always watching over

you are not here so only good or nothing happens to you at all

& you pass by this life without any action by simply sitting in your comfort zone

you will always be pushed forward,

even if you try to pass buy quietly or without harming any

life is not meant to be comfortable

you have to go to the further dimension so you need to evolve now,

if not consciously then unconsciously you will have to take the steps forward

& only after the disaster what you choose to do,

decides your next cycle or if you are ending it right now

so no matter how unconsciously you live your life but let the conscious mind take the decision for you

you are here for your soul's evolution

so don't attach yourself to the external

everything external to you is just here to trigger you for your growth and to make you comfortable while going through this process

so don't get over emotional for anything

whatever happens to you, learn your lesson and let it be.

61
Your say

"You & your fate is just one decision away"

Happiness is not a wish
but your enlightenment for things,
you need to have the eye, to value true life
awaken your conscious & leave everything behind
then you will find where true happiness lies
your journey, your life
you have to make it worth your time
it's your life on the plate
you eat or throw, it's your say
everyone has their decision to make
can you enjoy food,
if you have no teeth to chew?
so now is the time,
to go dig deeper in life
it's never too late to change sides
it is only for the bold to make
you & your fate is just one decision away
so think twice because
life is too precious to waste
you can use your time to create or waste
it's up to you, to acknowledge this fact
because even without you this life will go on

stressing & sadness will bring no values to it
even if you die today
life will still find its way
so break the cycles in which you live
& find a happier, meaningful way to exist.

62
Worth

"Energy of your spirit is more powerful than genetics & behavioral patterns"

Nobody can tell you your worth
it can't be taught
you have to put that value to yourself
nobody else can come and do that to you
embody it,
don't let anybody tell you your worth
feel that confidence, that worthiness in you
you will feel energetic & inspired
and a lot of thoughts need purification as well
find that fulfilment & go after what you want
fulfilment comes from energy, from what inspires you
that's what makes you happy
it is all there in you
don't let your ego, emotions or opinions blind you
you need to go through your door first
so you can enter in another room
then you will see the effort
and what you've accomplished throughout
that you did not recognize in you before
if you couldn't recognize something, then how can you value it?
stop the habit of people pleasing,

it is not honoring you
every person, situation & past only have lessons & value
it hurts,
but sometimes we go through the hurt to release energy
don't let anything ever that happened or happens to you, wall you up
because it blocks your heart
and all the creativity, comes through it
& you will block anything new that you want to create in the world
so healing & expansion of heart is necessary
with listening to your heart
spontaneity comes
energy flow increases
which in turn makes your creativity flow
so do the things that vibe with your soul
see the patterns in everything & flow through your dreams
don't feel paralyzed, when you're having a hard time
it takes a little too long sometimes
but it is a game of patience at that time
try seeing things full circle
it is better to wait for the harvest than to be impatient
what is in alignment with your soul & heart
that's all you need to pass through
when nothing seems logical
follow the logic of your spirit
perceive things from a higher level

live your truth
try to see things from a 5d plan
& remain calm in the chaos
see beyond time & space
life is a dance
only if you recognize the pattern in it
& unconditional love for anyone who comes across in this journey of who you are.

63
Procrastination

"Don't let your free will work against you, rather make it work for you"

Don't procrastinate your abundance
you're just delaying it because of your free will
you need to listen to your intuition
and believe in you & go for it with full strength
don't wait for a clear sign to do something
you need to trust yourself
if it aligns with your heart & soul,
if it makes you happy, go for it
to bring you to your fulfillment, build the energy to
break the loop and move forward
you are capable of doing that
be aware & get in tune with your intuition
trust it to guide you through all that
start using your free will to your advantage
understand how these life cycles work
there is no beginning or end to growth,
you are forever expanding
don't wait for the whistle to blow
stop tip toeing around the deeper emotion that you feel
stop cloaking yourself so you can't be fully seen
look at all your fears and banish them

it is about awakening of inner strength
come out with full expression of your inspiration, emotion and what sparks you
release your full creativity and move,
stop clutching out on ideas & your plans
grab your freaking broom & go in that direction
move away from the energy of avoidance & worries,
if we focus on the things that we don't have
then we are building on just keeping ourselves stuck
so focus on what you have, to move forward and let the rest follow
where there is movement there is growth
that's how you take back power & control
and let the momentum going so you can be unstoppable now
stop holding yourself back, embrace your confidence
don't confuse your comfort with your purpose
go deeper than just brushing off the surface
surrender the things that are out of your control and start the dance with all that you got
with pure utter confidence, that will allow you to grow
you don't need the fancy shoes or dress to dance,
you just need your feet
you don't have to be perfect before putting out your work in the world,
you are not too late or too young
you are great,
work on the closure of your past & fears
work for your success with honor & integrity

put in the work so you can harvest later
understand life on a deeper level so you can stop procrastinating your own abundance.

Triple moon goddess

64
Co-create

"Proclaim your light"

Be a fair leader
the fairest of the group,
no one is beneath you,
you may have more experience over someone else
so after you have set the intention
it's time to come into action
there is a time to be still
and then there is time to move forward
it's time to take the initiative now
though you have become comfortable in doing things on your own
& you love your solitude
but when its time,
know when to step out of your comfort zone
& go work with a group
you've already done so much by yourself
after putting the intention it's time to put action behind it
now to get working on your dreams, you need to involve others too
you need those extra resources & support to achieve your goals
break free from doing things on your own

(for the external achievements, dreams & goals)
so align with your soul's calling & find the real tribe for your job
hear your spirit,
get into attunement,
you are the queen of wands, never forget
she is the queen who goes out for what she wants
she accomplishes everything
she is also the collaborator
she has the ideas & knows how to work through
she is passionate
so integrate this part of yourself too
there is a time for waiting
but know, when to move forward
if anyone can, it's you, who can
for growth step out
you know what to do
hear your voice above any other, no matter how loud they are
that's how you work
don't lose yourself in a group
be the leader you're meant to
dignity is not something you can learn, get or demand
so work for your soul's calling with all that you got.

www.ingramcontent.com/pod-product-compliance
Ingram Content Group UK Ltd.
Pitfield, Milton Keynes, MK11 3LW, UK
UKHW040008200726
13854UKWH00001B/102

9 789354 721748